THE STRANGER MANUAL

THE STRANGER MANUAL

poems by
Catie Rosemurgy

Graywolf Press

Publication of this volume is made possible in part by a grant provided by the Minnesota State Arts Board, through an appropriation by the Minnesota State Legislature; a grant from the Wells Fargo Foundation Minnesota; and a grant from the National Endowment for the Arts, which believes that a great nation deserves great art. Significant support has also been provided by the Bush Foundation; Target; the McKnight Foundation; and other generous contributions from foundations, corporations, and individuals. To these organizations and individuals we offer our heartfelt thanks.

Published by Graywolf Press
250 Third Avenue North, Suite 600
Minneapolis, MN 55401
All rights reserved.

www.graywolfpress.org

Published in the United States of America

ISBN 978-1-55597-547-0

4 6 8 9 7 5 3

Library of Congress Control Number: 2009933817

Cover design: Kyle G. Hunter

Cover photo: Veer

for my girls

Contents

THE STRANGER MANUAL

Miss Peach Is a Cross Between

A missing tooth and a fang.
A bloom and a sandstorm.
A chain letter and a trapdoor.

A can opener and a kiss.
A moracca and a spear.

Lowered eyes and a suddenly somewhat disconcerting blow job.
A baroque flute flourish and an eerie silence just beyond the cabin wall.

A tube top and a biohazard mask.
Goldilocks and the tongue of a bear.

A little blackout on what you think was Tuesday
and a little black spot on your latest chest x-ray.

A little black period
that holds down words like a tack
and a bright little universe
that loves to turn black.

A Rose Is a Rose Is a Rose Is Miss Peach

You know that you think the flower is beautiful, but what else do you want to know
about the flower? What else can you know about the flower? What can you do to know
the flower? You can pick it, sketch it, wear it, put it in a vase. Hang it upside down
to dry it. Press it in a book, or read up on it in a book. You can write a book. You can get
access to a microscope. You can give it away. You can stand beside it and cry for
the brain's tendency to create beauty and then perceive it as unknowable. It isn't like
smashing your thumb, is it? So you pick the flower. It could be a daisy, but it might be
a rose, the kind of rose that has lived its entire life sipping the mist from the air, the kind
of rose that has a throat, a throat that is always moving, the kind that has petals you can
watch getting farther and farther apart and you can see growing more and more petals
in its center, the kind of rose you can watch until your head becomes heavy, saturated,
and exponential and starts to loll. It could be that kind of rose, and if it is,
do whatever you have to, but make it stop.

Miss Peach Goes Shopping

> *"Come buy, come buy."*
> Christina Rossetti

Miss Peach spends longer than necessary in the spinning door. She doesn't crash
into the tilted mannequins, but she looks as if she will. Liberté, fraternité, egalité,

my flammable sisters. Miss Peach has a spring catalog for a To Do list, and she moves her legs
like a prodigy. A hemline is one life decision best left to the faint of heart,

and Miss Peach never faints. No matter how she tries. She explains to several generations
of Princess-Cruise addicts behind the makeup counter that she's looking for a lip color

she can call Too Long in the Pool, or perhaps Why Did I Eat That? Her face is bound
to keep popping up here and there, underneath her lover and behind

the things she says. Beauty is for maple trees. When people look at her,
Miss Peach wants each of them to worry: wait a second, did I just beat her up?

Miss Peach's sighs yellow slightly. The luxury-car collectors behind the makeup counter
don't understand. OK, a metaphor, she says, I want to look like your reflection

in a mirror after dark. One of them gets it, leans back as if into a director's chair.
So eye shadow, she says, is a way of taking on the night and making sure that you lose.

Miss Peach's work here is nearly done. She feels game for anything,
like when she finds a window she can climb out, even though it's dark

and she's not familiar with the layout of the room. The other sprinkler-owner
behind the makeup counter is lit up like a button on a suicide hot line. She says,

you know what people want in their mouths: the too hot strudel, the questionable shrimp.
Miss Peach lets her foundation run. Her face is underneath, after all, peeking through

like a rock through cut grass. With the help of the misunderstood artists
behind the makeup counter, Miss Peach buys herself a rosier nipple, a new front tooth,

some pseudo bruises, and a crown, a golden crown that will snag your skin if you ever
try to touch it and will keep you right next to her.

Neighbor: Miss Peach's Body Didn't Turn Out Right

But whose did? She's crumpled where she's supposed to be unfolded,
something bad written on a piece of paper. Her walking
is a devolution that hunches and shrinks everyone

as she moves up the tree-lined street. I'm on my porch waving to neighbors
and having one of those honeyed afternoons when I don't know who I am.

I know everything else, though, and it's ringing in my head. Then there she is
in a pool on my front steps, laughing, asking about lunch, as if the bones
of at least four different animals weren't loose inside her, scurrying this way and that.
Someone needs to find her a place to live, a hidey hole we can cram food in
and get away from quickly. We could call her part bird

and be done with it. But everyone is dying right under the surface these days,
especially around the eyes. Death has crawled up into the face
to nibble away whatever blocks its view of the stars.
We're riddled with it. It's pulling our flesh

into outrageous, unwilled positions, like the huge smile on my face
as I lift her onto my lap and hold her together for a minute
before I tell her she isn't welcome here.

First Day Out

A man looks good pushing against the air
and is a winter fruit.

A woman looks good rounding out the flat light
and is a summer fruit. Goodbye and hello
to all I haven't eaten.
                    I'm slumped by the converted garage
unable to survive without specialized machinery.
                              Grandeur tugs at the sky,
rearranges the buildings,
flecks the brick and the sidewalk with bits of fusion.
As always, the first thing I need
is a colorful collection of bowls.
                  My breath in a sack and my legs dragging aquatically behind me,
I'm crawling to the party I've always dreamed of.
It is utterly worth it. Doors and curbs look on,
epic and glacial. Concrete and dirt
have been badly misrepresented.
                            Living is imprecise.
                  The end is about light, but not in the way
history has imagined. Anything blinding and unknown
we recognize immediately as our new home.

All Objects Reveal Something about the Body

Crisp is to the apple what
flexed is to the body.

Poor apple.

Being bitten is to the crisp apple
what walking is to the ripe body, but it's more complicated than that:

the apple of the face has been given
to the running juice of the body

and the body, which is often gracious,
makes it shine.

Lucky apple.

Having a core is to the apple
what having a core is to the body, city, method, circumstance, endeavor.

Having a core is flower-shaped and hurts
in the way that having a shape hurts, which is to say

it hurts ironically, because to have limits
is not just to make a declaration upon a mountainside,

it is also to be the mountainside. Having a flowering core
also hurts in the way that being flower-like always hurts,

which is to say sexually, as if the whole self
has exceeded the skin, which it hasn't, which means

we always seem to be opening but never do.
Both these types of suffering color the air

when we pause to have them. The affected atoms
are hard to see among the billions

of sofa atoms and newsprint atoms
but, like the illnesses in the crystalline sea, they are there.

Red apple, sliced, quartered, salted. Green apple,

alone in the basket.
Anything left on the shelf becomes weak,

suggestible, vulnerable to other shapes, hungry,
a poison apple.

The joining we do with others needs containing.

Apple pie.
Imagine the mess. Imagine a finger touching the sack of the heart.

Imagine nothing that powerful
being possible, nothing ever stopping you

at the root of the breath. Huge apple.
The world in reference to you. Time a backdrop.

Or close the other eye: you in reference to the world.
How it varies and happens simultaneously.

Good morning.
Little apple.

Miss Peach Imagines She Is an Aging British Rock Star and Explains What Honesty Is

At the base of my wet brain—whatever,
of all brains, all allegedly intricate human brains—
a smallness lies tangled in the roots
of largeness, the one interesting secret is lost

inside the big idea. At least I, in my red socks, hope so.
Though I, in my satin coat, suppose not.
Am I, cross-legged in a chair, floating high
in an undisclosed and perfumed location,

refusing to speak to you in a glamorous city,
fairly analogous to it?
Not even remotely.
Nor is the sun, nor is the seed.

Nor is the city at all glamorous.
But there is the need, sometimes at least,
to taste—whatever,
a good grape— when all alone.

To double over or just bend a bit
as if in ecstasy because one is stuck
with one's self and with what it's like
to have one's mouth full.

Or perhaps there isn't
such a need per se, or perhaps the labs
haven't yet found it. But there is
such a grape, and it has

broken my heart. Nothing else has.
And when I forget that you are here
asking what it means to be too old
for all this having and doing that is

unseemly and the opposite of dying,
when I hate you as much as I can
when I am not stupid and know it might be
me I hate or today and not you, exactly,

and when I run my hand along
the thread of my coat and realize
that in this light the fabric really is
an extraordinarily menacing yellow,

the color of diseased royalty run amok,
of a swollen and unnatural skin
forming around the sun,
I feel a freedom

about the size of a dime
inside my head, where no one
can find it, and, like wind through
a bullet hole, it sings to me.

The Wondering Class

I think the stomach means we cannot love one another properly.

I think the stomach is our one true eye.

I think the stomach is an ingredient.

I think the fingers mean we are too small inside one another.

I think the fingers mean our roots became bone and we lurched away
with a new agenda.

I think the eyelash means we can float to the ground like snow.

I think the eyelash means we must not appear burned.

Some of us have been burned, but that is not what the eyelash means.
It is unprepared for. It is the other side of the world.

The other side of the world is intricate with the lace of forests.

The other side of the world is a euphemism for disease.

I think disease means the cells have rearranged to mirror something fast and jagged
approaching from the sky.

I think disease means full expression.

I think disease means the river truly was as golden as it seemed.

Gold River Is Never Really on Fire

There is wolf behavior here. Families around fires,
packs at safe distances. Just like the stars,
we make sense in groups. When asked about trees,

some say that branched things are lies
we've been telling about ourselves for years.
Some say you can't walk by a thing flooded with sugar
and not know yourself better. Some say we are fire to things
that just want to be wooden.

There are sticks here and boys and always
a stone or a clod of earth that can be turned into a ball.
There are water sounds coming from the dark pool of ink
with which our pines were drawn. There are forked branches we are like
and forked branches we aren't. There are hundreds

of small toads on the ground, and it doesn't matter
what the toads are trying to do
because they don't know how to do it.

Even in the dark we throw and catch with one another so well
a system is revealed. We're rich
with hubs of the wheel. The lake, the moon, the ball,
the shining necklace of our faces that the night wears.

When we walk back to the circle, the fires split each of us in half,
neatly at last, into what can be lit up
and what obviously cannot.

Miss Peach Returns to High School to Retake Driver's Ed

One cannot love something
one has too much power over, such as cars
and younger men. This is not to imply too much

of a similarity between cars, which emit
a greenish light from their control panels,
and educated younger men, who have
pretty eyes. Both tend to crash,

but whose fault is that? All one can do
is roll down the window and try
to avoid legal prosecution.
Which is not to say younger men are too much

younger or smarter, or more visionary,
or that cars are necessarily
insane-making. One is not so susceptible,
and one is not sickening. Such a thought, in fact,
makes one spit. Rule-making becomes impossible
when one is disgusting, and life is about making

and being made by forces
which one knows are there, even if
one cannot see them
being drawn in the sand. Life is not about

personality disorders. Yet slowness remains,
one learns through reading,
a cultural crisis. The movies can't figure it out.
Given our endless but civic pretending,

some rare, muscled, or differently fueled thing
must at least convincingly
play the role of speed. America, one sings in school,

is the great process of careening
into the unknown. Being American,
one hopes, is the flattering process
of having one's hair blown back.
This is what is true about otherwise
stupid love. But the powerless, vaguely mint-flavored
younger man is not here
solely to meet up at 5 A.M. before practice.

Look at the beautiful blurring
of his pre-important edges.
One cannot reside in a dewy nation of becoming
without wanting to wake up

married to whatever sweet,
smart thing hasn't happened yet. Oh, steering wheel.
Oh, gas pedal. You are terrible lies.
Oh, pretty eyes. Pretty, visionary, bewildered eyes.
Where in the hell are we going?

Doctor: Miss Peach Is a Doll inside a Doll inside a Doll

When she lay down as if to go to sleep,
I mentioned I had another client to meet.
I requested that we continue our talk later next week.
I asked her to leave and, finally, told her to get out. She sat up and said
that she's the pretty mute holding daisies who we're all looking for
as we peel away the layers and layers of girls.
She said she meant
that friends are like magic tricks
but love is genuinely pulling someone in half. It's as if no one
even has hands anymore, she said. She said she wasn't bragging,
she glows at the center of god knows what like a jewel.
No amount of mining could exhaust the riches.
It's the same with me and the same with the universe
and the same with a flower, but no one ever twists hard enough.

She said she had invented a tool. She said not to worry,
there are glitches, but she's working them out on herself.
The main problem is when someone looks at her:
it's like being born and then born and then born
but never being able to take her first breath.
She asked if I was committed to my current system of breathing. My right side lit up
with a burning pain. The best description I can offer for what happened next
is that my head became one color in a large rainbow. I woke up here.

Gold River

The arch in the bridge. The moment of architecture.
The island where you lost your mother's keys. The photo she sent
of someone who looks like her walking to the point
where the land becomes reminiscent of dissolving of flesh.
The trees stamped onto our minds like traumas
are supposed to be. The frightening blanks where the stores were.
The sense the owners died. How many people killed by logs,
do you think, over the years? The moon sitting greedily
on your house. The carrying of one another
when young, light, and poisoned. The doorsteps
we were left on. The fox scat. The extra points in school. Who knew
how prominently quarries featured? Only once or twice in a lifetime
does one find the suicide or hear the primordial screaming. The towns nearby
that survive on museums of their earlier burning. The dreams set
in neighbor's houses. The mounds with hooves and bones sticking out.
The gentle sloping. We will always be swimmers
digging into the thaw. The former newness. The various cuts of meat.
The places cats won't go. The climbing out onto riverbanks. Like a milkweed
or a fox you are something that parted the dirt here. The rotting
that sets in when you leave.

Love, with Trees and Lightning

I've been thinking about what love is for.
Not the obvious part where he gathers
until he is as purposeful inside her
as an electrical storm, not when he breaks
into a thanks so bright it leaves her
split like a tree. (We all jolt back,
our picnic ten shades lighter, our hands
clapped over awe that's too big for our mouths.)

But the two of them, afterwards,
tasting the electricity, nibbling
the charge on the ions. When her pulse
has already risked coming to meet him
at the window of her skin. When what is left
of his body still feels huge, and he sits draped
in his fine, long coat of animal muscles
but uses all his strength to be almost imperceptible.
They curl up, make their bodies the same size,
draw promises in one another's juices.
"You," they say. I love it when they say that.

Would that they could give a solid reason.
Sometimes they even refuse to try.
They make jokes while cinching their laces.
"I'll call soon," he says. "You're so sweet,"
she says, but the rank sugar of his breath
doesn't summarize the world for her.
"Not you," they say.

And nothing bad has happened.
They just turn the doorknob that has been
shining in their hands the whole time, walk out,
and continue to die. Same as the rest of us.
So maybe love is a form of crying. Or maybe
it's our way of finishing what the leaves have started
and turning a brilliant color before we hit the ground.
Name one living thing that doesn't somehow bloom.
None of them get to choose the right conditions.
Think of chemical fires or ghost orchids.

Maybe one body is simply insufficient.
So they change their minds and decide
to stand by one another's side for years.
They bring flowers and carpet and children
into the act. They refuse to move, ever.
They act as if they've found the only hospitable
spot on earth. I love it when they do that.

Doctor (2): Miss Peach Seeks Treatment at the Rural Walk-in Clinic

At first she refused to sign in, even with her face seeping like a steak
thrown into the snow. "Pink eye," she said. "Scum at the back of the head.
Brain dirt. Oh," she said, patting my breasts, "pretty, pillowed nurse," even though
she knows I'm a doctor. "No," I said,

"You've been playing with ill children again. You've been
their real mother again in the woods." Sick heart.
As if I know what on earth a heart is.

As usual, I braided her hair. She winked at me and suckled
at the thermometer. Fluid that was not quite tears
dripped from her chin. Poor science,

it tries so hard that it misses the obvious: at first her body is an abandoned nest.
I should know. Once again amid the hush of vials, she came together briefly
like a pile of twigs and held me. A field grew
out of the damp and quiet. I closed the door, walked down,
and bathed in the river of her staring.

Neighbor(2): Miss Peach in Velvet

The relationship among objects was planetary, the air
slightly yellow. My robe, maroon. Wife and kids,
still sleeping. The hum of the foreign brain stem

was hard to hear, the fur and bone
of a rippling animal, heat covered in velvet.

A whitetail buck will occasionally look right at you
in late winter or early spring before the fighting starts.
At last to see the eyes you've always wanted for your own head.

So what a mockery
to find a shrunken woman in a costume,
a neighborhood joke, a cake with antlers.
It is foolish to feel worthy of a god.

She breathed wetly against my skin, intermittently
as if she were injured.

I admit I stroked her matted, massive neck
until she slept. I knew the comfort of having hollows
in which millions of other things live.

She asks only that I stand a few minutes in the clearing,
arms stretched out, open to ridicule.
She licks me with her wind-scented mouth and purrs,
moos, chirps, bleats.
I know what vines know.

She lowers her great horns,
folds her crusted wings.

Summer in Gold River

Our town squishes like a pillow against our cheeks.
Its coolness is the best river. We have the best life,
the best wind, the best large birds. We cannot be bitten
by the teeth that are everywhere. We've built a roof
on each of our triumphs. We are also lucky in these ways:
radiance is the most lovely harbinger of death,
and it feels as if the clouds have been wrung from our hearts.
We have the best sense of compressing life
into simple greetings here. Some people have asked the question,
what is a bad sign? I'm considered a type of child
but I say it's when people you love go missing.
And yet, curled up each night at the end of our yard
is a faded lake sent as a gift from another world.
We swim in it once the work of watching the sun stay whole
is truly over. We've survived as a species
mainly because of the dripping. It's best if our skin
is alive and moving when we head through the trees,
when we stop on our path to sniff the air like dogs.
It's best that it's dark, and that we're no longer sure
if what we are bathed in is actually water.

In Defense of the Prince of Gold River

Given, only after attending several state-sponsored floodings
did he begin saving the thinned-haired children in earnest.
Meanwhile, he changed the color of his royal standard three times.

But the children were rosy-cheeked, pocked, dim, reeking
of piss and whatever they could smoke. They had their fingers
inside one another and were drooling. He floated in on a barge

made to look like a lotus. He had a small library unloaded onto the shore
and said books were like tongues cut out of great men.
Some of the children grabbed a copy, ran off, and were never seen again.
One or two were found nailed to trees, but others have breezes
named after them.

What does that prove? They could be eating tourtière on a porch right now.
You act as if you've never held their prickly stand-in dolls and felt safe.

We were ugly and like the mad center of a blossom he looked at us.

From the other side of the river, the children flash lights
at the five of us who are left. They send their loose hairs to us on the wind
so we can weave them into a way out.*

* I injected a fat twinkling into his blood, particulate and cruel, the sharpened edges
  of which we will soon rue if we decide to burn him.

The Groundwork

As always, when one part is missing, it represents your belonging,
sacrificed with a disturbing neatness.

Consider the acoustic guitar: very sad.
Another moaning, polished object calling to its missing piece.

As if wholeness wouldn't mean the end of the music.
As if it wouldn't mean you were ridiculous
on the sofa, wrapped around a few slats of wood.

Let's uncork the small bottles of death and let them breathe. Give us
an obvious, basic danger, like a fire,
that a family can gather around. Look,

out the wall-sized window where the lake was. The night loves you

and is pressing its blue-black heart against the glass.
You've been taken away from something enlarged with need
and caused it to sing as well.

Miss Peach, Female Impersonator

Call me gloomy,
but does he love me because I'm low calorie?
Because I resemble a particular statue
but can move my tongue?

Call me Cassandraic,
but aren't we getting a bit comfortable
with being plain, with being shown up by small birds
and their braggart little names?

Call me stingy,
but the world is hardly a stage. It's too cluttered
with trees. Especially the budding ones.
They always steal the dying scenes.

Call me romantic,
but don't I have a lover here somewhere?
Underneath all these eyelashes
and Daisy razors?

Call me sentimental,
but remember that time I was born?
Opening my mouth came so naturally to me.
And what an outfit. Cosmic spill.

Call me naïve,
but like everyone else I'm a sucker
for being held close and absolved of weaknesses
I don't necessarily have.

Call me optimistic,
but I believe that inside every girl
is someone who is not a girl
but who looks like one and laughs.

Call me closer is all. By a name
you've made up just for me. Little Pistachio.
Dull Meat, Colored Shell. Name anything
you like and look harder. Call me that, too.

Miss Peach Explains Promiscuity to a Toddler

Say this yellow square block is bored. Say she's bored because she's always been
a yellow square block and has always been knocked down with other yellow square blocks.
So one day she goes to the couch where she meets some blue rectangles. The idea
is to make something she hasn't seen fall down before. When she gets her hands on her
first blue rectangle, she can't keep from examining it. She examines many and figures
she'll never tire of it. One of the rectangles strikes her as unusually blue. To you and me
it might not look that different from the other blue rectangles, but she likes it so much,
as if it is far superior. It might as well be far superior. She enjoys this discovery.
She wants to go further across the carpet. She wants another chance to make something
superior just by liking it.

Miss Peach Visits Her Ex-Boyfriends in the Hospital

Oh, fellas, unfortunately, we have no more time
for unintelligible moaning. When your shoes
are as narrow as mine, it's one thing
to say something and another to actually think it,

and I often think I love you guys,
with your broken optical blood vessels

and the different parts of each of you that will be
shrunken and hairy when the casts come off.
Yes. It's clear what's been taken. It's almost

as if someone who can pass for no one
has been sneaking in late, when only
the monitor lights are still awake, and ineffectually
sucking the life out of you, getting only as far

as Stephen's forearm, Joe's left ankle, Rodney's neck.
So, yes, Halleluja. Poor Dan will walk again. If there is
a Big Void, a Mighty Abyss, a Sudden Chasm,
then it only nicked you.

But where does that leave the five of us?
You are not merely a red wire inserted where
a black wire should have been. I do believe
you have your own arbitrary
likes and dislikes, your own sensory responses

that you do or do not find reliable. Don't get me wrong,
I would surely vote for any one of you
if you were running for the City Council, or even
if you were just running, say from a burglar you inadvertently caught
by glancing out the kitchen window.
What I'm trying to say

is that I'm behind you all the way. And I mean that
in its most innocuous sense.
Because that's what love is, after all, isn't it?
The nagging, guilty feeling you get after
you wish someone were dead.

Winter in Gold River

Pretty girl. The weather has knocked her down again
and given her to the lake to wear as a skin.

Why am I always being the weather?
There were days in the winter
when her smile was so lovely I felt
the breathing of my own goodness,

though it remained fetal and separate.
I was a scavenger who survives

with a sling and stones, but whose god
nonetheless invents the first small bright bird.
And it was like flight to bring food to her lips

with a skeletal hand. But now she will always
be naked and sad. She will be what happens

to lake water that is loved and is also
shallow enough. The thickening, the slowing,
the black blood of it, the chest opened
to reveal the inevitable heart attack.

God, the silence of the chamber
we watch from. What happens to water
that isn't loved? It undergoes processes.

It freezes beside traffic.
But the reaching out to all sides at once,
the wet closing of what was open?
That is a beautiful woman.

So of course I stand and stare, never able
to pinpoint the exact moment I killed her.

Monday in Gold River

Everyone knows trees are bodies, yet another
x-ray of wanting and we've already seen

too many of those. Winter, on the other hand,
is always mind, and the combination is Monday

or 7:13 P.M. or an indeterminate source
of hunger which we must walk through

just to get to the store. There are, at least,
many confusing parts to each day:

who to love, what to cry for, whether or not
to read, where, fundamentally, to shit.

And there are a hundred potential
sources of pain where the ground

used to be. The result of things
being whole is parts and of things

being parts is wholes. In other words,
one tight red berry is shaking

on the vine. This town's gleaming
is the result of frost and the newly ominous

noise of footsteps. The mind walks with the body
on the body's own breaking.

The body carries the mind over the shattering
that lurks in its own frozen field.

The Prince of Gold River on the Imposition of the Galactic

In the age of the stars, everything.
Piles of everything. The ratios and temperatures

are perfect. Why, in this universe, do boiling points
and cosmic speed limits feel like a warning?
Why does symmetry gape like a trap,
as if two matching children are about to be devoured?

I am the steam rising off a charging horse.
I am an injured pair of horns.
At the end of a long hallway, I am still and unavailable.

Count this among your sorrows:
I have taken the housetops.
Whatever the night's been made of all this time
will soak right into you.

Make a note in my journals: how seditious the moon,
how exquisite the moisture.

I have ruled this country as well as I could
with death and feathers as my only tools.

Miss Peach: The War Years

She's been lobbed,
and like the other grenades
can't help but like
the deeply American ache
where the pin used to be.
She is a squat,
angry seed that blooms
into absence, into big flowers
of what was, a trick fruit
that creates its own mouth,
a wild eye that blinks
its own face away. Luckily,
she feels only the slightest tingle
of the empiricism, of the impact she'll have
wherever she lands.
She's had to insinuate herself
into everything else: the concept
of time, the elaborate and ruthless
culture of love, the life cycle
of trees. But the space that must be
cleared for her, the threat
she poses to other living things,
this is her radius.

Miss Peach: The College Years

I. Pledge Sister

Everyone looks at me as if I'm a rainbow
drawn by a slow child. Because they can eat without
a ringing in their ears. They can ask for gravy.
They miss the point I'm always
aiming at their heads. The pills I suck are like me:
pink, fizzy, and totally legal. They turn listening to noise
into a type of eating.

Everyone wants to know about my pubic hair.
They say they're looking for signs that I'm dying,
but what they really want is the food melting on the fork
when they finally say *none for me, thanks.* They worship
the pain they think I'm in. Meanwhile,
I'd eat a beetle if I thought its legs
could make my lashes longer. I've got all these
organs inside me and I can't resist teasing them
to see if they'll go away.

Everyone likes it when I finally die in the magazine article:
the cries no one heard, the love I needed massaged
into my hamburger meat. No one knows I am the flower,
the bee, the wind, the rain, the dirt: all the vectors.
No one knows how well I sleep, how well I lie in bed
not sleeping. I run and sharpen
the bones of my face. The other girls say
they don't care if their shadows aren't museum quality. They're happy
just knowing they're made of marble. They have no respect
for the chisel I would take to the human race.

II. Spring Break

Love isn't above starting this way:
you can drop me from a second-story window
if you pin me against it first. It doesn't want to start this way,
and who can blame it. There's the electric outlet and then
there's the baby finger stuck into it. I was both.

A couple nights later, on a busy street, I recognized his walk
the way a mouse must recognize the hole it used last winter.
Sure, I wish the universe would clear its throat.
Sure, I'm sick of the source of great fire
always being the sun. A few nights ago he peeled off of me
as if he were my own skin and he didn't want the job.

But afterwards he kissed me as if to apologize
for every brutal thing he was strong enough to have just done.
Later he walked me across town, and we ended up
in an expensive place, in the middle
of a loud song. He looked right at me
the whole time, as if I were still the one thing he would choose,
even though the damn thing couldn't stop spinning
and was clearly broken.

III. The Essay

It is dumb to know what one has longing for.
I am moved by the orange stitching on a girl's corduroy book bag.

I, too, wonder what I am happy about.
There is always something natural in pieces

like sand or snow. If early Western cultures
had perceived the surface of the day as wrapping around them like a shell,
I wouldn't be here right now.
Not exactly me, not exactly here, not exactly now. The world spreads out

from how we look at one thing. I tell myself this and then I look at things for hours.

Don't think I don't know how stupid I sound. Please, do not think I don't know.

IV. Fifth-Year Senior

Everything tastes like love. That's what
makes me nervous. That and I wish I knew what I will act like

later today. I watch myself being kind sometimes
and I think, is there nothing you won't fake?

But that's unforgiving. A smile, a purse, an ax,
these are all things you pick up and carry.

Lately, I pick up the lightest things. I am floating and honored
to drag myself back and forth like a huge feather

across my sleeping boyfriend. He thanks me
by actually changing under my touch. He is smooth

and I worry that I barely feel him,
but doing things no one should see

seems the only good use of my time. He buys me
jewelry I never wear. I love it because it piles up, which proves

I'm alive. The boys my age cry more than the girls do.
They're always losing games, and those are very symbolic.

My girlfriends and I can't get off the couch anymore,
and summer is seeping in under the doors.

My friend says people are wrong about us.
It's the ripe fruit that gets eaten. I say the truth is

I don't work at things because then
I get them.

V. Graduation Address

I like to be at the end and look back
at the beginning and see all
the stupidity there.

I think we are young.
The posters all say so,
and though no one ever officially
joined our clubs, we designed many logos.

The beautiful, dumb girl you loved
was everyone at our lecture,
and what a strange boy we all were in the corner
with our walking stick, talking too much
about the board games back home.

Many of you were next to me at the talk where I became
hyper-aware of the creeping in my heart.

As you know, I became obsessed
with the on and off inside my chest.

Failure seems to be one half of the deal, which is why
I have occasionally climbed on top of some of you
and then left the room. But there is another way
to look at it: like you, I am a house

for a wet animal that is sneaking up
on something it is terrified by. What is that something?
The wet animal doesn't know.
The wet animal doesn't even have eyes.
There's no way that wet animal isn't brave.

Things That Didn't Work

Touching, seriousness, snow.
The short list of lovers anyone has ever had, both of whom
have turned into long, quiet rivers.

Geraniums and their bruises that ruin
the clean edges of summer. The mother wiping
her son's cheek with spit.

Picture frames. Targets. The psychological
boundaries described in books.
Any shape or line whatsoever.

New Year's Eve

The lake wouldn't let us in. We had to walk on it
like a family of children talking to a mother's grave.

The snow lifted from the ice like a face
breaking apart. Our own skin held tight
but smelled crushed

like mint. The wind had licked the sky clean,
but then we showed up with our pulses

tucked in gloves. We stood out
against the blankness like creatures
that needed to be studied. Even the color
of my cousin's jacket was portentous.

If it were summer, we would've sunk,
and we would've done it anyway.

What had crawled into our hearts?
We were losing track of one another
and the shore. My aunt appeared briefly
and touched my cheek. The night had hardened
and gotten heavier. The stars dropped it.

We were sent to witness our inability to pick it up.
We were our true selves briefly.

Miss Peach Pierces the Vale

I am the bowl that holds the light that the Lord will bring to His face
and use as His eyes.

I've imagined not knowing my purpose.
Such a person must lie awake among the objects in her room.

She must choose her behaviors carefully around handicapped children.
When anyone smiles, touches her softly, leans in
to test the atrophied appendage, she must think she has made
some difference to them. As if every person she met that day had stopped breathing
and she'd been found in the nick of time, lying around, common as a pen,
and just happened to be the perfect instrument
for getting air into their blocked throats.

Later we will learn that the man whistling from his new mouth
had not, in fact, been choking.

The field is bare. The grasses are simple gestures, curved lines, and they bend
to indicate when the Lord is near and giving off heat.
Catch the walls of the day off-guard and they waver like water. An eye is burning
through the fluid that surrounds it. The earth is floating
in the socket, and the body is the empty pupil of its hot looking.
A pen could slip in it, and there would be no blindness.

The grasses teach us to be simple and curved. The grasses take over
the trembling. They hold the looking that spills into seeing. The grasses are blessed,
inadequate vessels. I must walk through them.
My footsteps will soon be fire.

And They Can No Longer Die, for They Are Like Angels

Have you ever been in church or temple

and thought, OK.
Then you know my sister.

And maybe your sister.
But mostly mine. She will crush you.

But in this photo she teaches the sun to set itself down on the merciful water

in pieces at our feet.
That is an impossible thing to do.

That is the aforementioned
weird feeling in church. But get your own sister.

Get a house and unleash
your allotment of consequences. Finger the thin skin

of the infant head that seals in
that which is not you.

Rock and hum because there are no words.
It's not my sister,

but it's a start. Note the scar
where the silver cat scratched her bud of a nose which proves

she's about becoming. Now know her face
as a sign of where you don't go. Live quietly

with your strange blood inside your tongue waiting to flower.

Take whatever is sharp in you and walk in the other room.
Dull it now on the rock of your own sister.

New York, New York, New York, New York, New York

Our heads too big for us,
our laugh, hands, sex too big for us,

we're coming, dragging excess skin that looks,
in dim light, like flowers. Coming

to tear you down whenever
our eyes close. Coming,

when they startle open,
to have failed. That's what need is now:

grabbing and then checking to see
what it is you are holding.

We want only the bold and shapeless,
only the rare as in bloody.

We don't know what it is.
It rings, though, and can afford

to be made of glass. The people around us
sharpen slowly like teeth

in a mouth so crowded
it must remain open.

That is what we must stand in,
the dark rooms and the bright,

the little girls and their absence.
We're bringing the symphonies

we can finally mount onto our violins.
We're coming to be so nearly pierced

by buildings that miss us all around. Soon
we won't know anything

but that thrill. We'll eat
and not know what we've eaten.

We'll lie in dark liquids and whisper to you
of our swelling.

Miss Peach Imagines She Is an Aging British Rock Star and Considers the Human Condition While Responding to a Beautiful Woman Who Has Just Said "I Love You"

It's OK to feel important.

The swelling between our legs
indicates we are rare flowers.

We bloom in the most
idiosyncratic conditions: rubber,

misery, great shoes. The other day

I realized that we can't spit
without hitting grass or something else

that implies the necessity
of our experience, of our greatness.

We can control what we want to grow in our yards.

We have developed capillaries shaped like ferns
shaped like trees shaped like lightning

shaped like math shaped like . . .

What more is there to say? Nothing, but, my god,
listen to us. The whole sky was the inspiration

for our hearts—otherwise,
we wouldn't have such dark hearts.

The obvious tinyness of the stars

is even better proof. Almost all our books argue
that even those footnotes, those glints

off the night's teeth are bigger than us.
Tell me, who else but the enormous

could risk writing such books?

Miss Peach and the Problem of Human Beauty

I agree with the central conclusion of all pop songs: you're gorgeous
and I'm angry. You walked into the party like the last thing you'd ever do
was walk onto a yacht. In the hospital,

I had time to consider the ever-so-slightly corrupt taste of your freshly cleaned armpits.
I was always feverish to pry the full smell of you back open. Perhaps stink,
in our antiseptic culture,

is the greatest intimacy. I thought about what the nurse couldn't bring me,
about morphine and your eyes. Eyes so pure yet so in your defiled head. There it is,
that complexity in my stomach. So beyond

science, so worthy of mysticism, so impossible to experience and continue standing.
If God did anything, he invented a shapelessness rigged to get sick of itself immediately.
This sadness evolved into human beings

who pit their meticulous fingers against various centuries. Formalism, on earth,
became addictive, funny, tender. It developed into the elaborate
problem of your eyes and their aesthetic

relationship to the rings inside an old, glowing tree. I had some dreams,
they were clouds in my coffee, clouds in my coffee, but, like all symmetrical, autumnal
maple leaves, your body is going to be used

experimentally to contact God. Because God is the most extreme case of a lot of people
feeling like I do about you: to imagine touching you should be the same as touching you.
Because if God weren't just the moment between

shapelessness and shape, he would've been one sly dog. Some people might've said
he was shallow based on things like you and sunsets, but I would've said,
let's try to be more hopeful:

if God weren't just a bearded embodiment of our misguided faith in cognition,
then he'd be the kind of supernatural presence that would die trying. But since he is
just a brain chemical and since we are

nonetheless surrounded by something large as it dies trying, then that must be
what *we* are, God as he enters the final stages and loses control of the muscles
in his own face. And in that way, we're all so damn beautiful.

The Monkey Whose Job It Used to Be to Sit on Miss Peach's Shoulder Takes Up Olde Timey Music

There is a cartoon about everything
I've ever done.
Whoa   whooooa whoa

Remember the episode
about the tiny banjo the pink-gummed monkey thumps
plink   plink   plink   with his dirty nails?

The Easter special about his one good friend being gone?

I wait by the petal-sick river
for the hatred to subside. My belly at least
is soft to me and kind
in the way of getting full. Most things never doooooooooooo.

Have you ever woken up sideways with a small carcass and fleas
only to become the inspiration for all flowers made of other tiny flowers
the very next day?
Strum   strum   strum

The past is not so bad.
It's full of lights.
Chord   chord   chord

Like the past, the monkey sleeps in the trees at night
under an unflinching moon and brushes
his own smart, flying tail.
Tittledy   tittledy   tooooooooooooooooo In the morning

sweet sunshine between his hairs
is no crime. When you wake up and there's his big smile that seems
very borrowed,
please remember:
he learned it from yoooooooooooooou

Most Loss Takes Place at the Cellular Level

Though from the way Monica (aka Kimmy
aka Guinevere) is bleeding from the eyes
you wouldn't think so. Her man (Vice President
in charge of patchy body hair) has officially
resigned amid allegations of staring
at all the wrong things. Let's get a test sample
of the remains dripping down the walls:
tomato paste, possible feces, lipstick, mint.
The emotions have grown listless
in their cages, the luster of hair and eyes has stiffened
like concrete. Fourth down and ten to go.
Captain Peppercorn—so named
because of the preciousness of lumpy things
and because in the end he is best ground up—
has been called to Fort Beautiful for duty.
No matter. Not two weeks later, Monica
(aka George Hammerstein aka Tupak) has perfected
the scarfed nonchalance of infidels and no longer
believes in systems, nevermind ritualized
genital flower performatives. The days after
the 2027 Domestic Let's Get Real Act have become
harder to fill but otherwise Tupak aka Fredrick
Von Monicastein aka Nick Miller from 3B can only
smile inwardly at his sick former reliance
on what it was like to touch her. OK, sometimes
he loses his footing in a split second revelry
of hair and spit and shopping for celery, but he rights himself
quickly, raises his ice ax, digs in his crampons,
and screams louder than before, in tandem with the others,
Conquistadors, people! Methodologies! A sort of reversible fabric!
Golden treasure! Epistemological unease!
Once he was left for years in a colorless room,
empty of everything but a steel wire

and a power outlet. Now on only the coldest days,
blind and close to the summit, does he sting himself
with private images: each of her fingers
burrowed inside him, his pet name for her entire hand.
Oh, the race to escape while still touching,
the secret ways out, the blocked tunnels,
light seeping in. The brief spots of radiant time
left out of the official report.

Doctor(3): Miss Peach Is Referred to the Orthopedic Unit

Patient presents with an alternating overabundance
and absence of bones. An inquiry into the patient's lifestyle

is conducted to explore possible environmental factors.
Patient claims to be twelve years old

and is 3'4", biscuit-shaped, powdery,
but incredibly adept at climbing trees.

Patient complains of electric knee caps
and says she can prove she's female.

She is currently under investigation for a series
of thefts involving stay-at-home mothers

forced to watch as she makes sandwiches and tries
to pour herself a glass of honey. She asks the victims

to give her their favorite t-shirts and tickle her
under the chin. Patient compares the pain

in her various spines to the plots and sub-plots
of an unread novel and her state of mind

to the unexpected emotional response
one has to the English countryside.

Patient resides in the woods behind the mall
in a lean-to she says she fashioned from gum

and the world's unremitting charity.
She collects hobo sacks and ointments that she hopes will

help her sleep while her bones come and go.
Patient asks repeatedly to sit on my shoulder.

She says she likes her ice cream the same way I do.
She has the eyes of an eagle who has learned kindness.

Patient convulses violently but attempts to hide it
by crossing her legs. Consequently her teeth chip.

Pulse 110. Blood pressure 70/40.
Eyes glassy. Smile leaky. Glands swollen. Face currently missing.

What Will Become of This Tension

The little girls appeared like stains in Miss Peach's tidy room. She worked to get rid of one, but they were always two. She broke any mirror that could have been responsible, yet still they remained, like statues remain in churches and eyes remain in heads. Their hands were slippery like something they should throw away. They made one another hungry for things like buttons they didn't know how to eat. Miss Peach, they said, your watching makes us play all the roles. Eventually the day fell off as inconsequentially as a finger, and they were gone. Only the lifelessness of her dolls stayed with her. She fed on it as long as she could.

A Poem about Poetry by Miss Peach, Hobo/Provocateur

Note: If there's one thing people in the world love it's a poem about poetry. Poems about poetry are like bowls of sequined fake fruit—you can't eat 'em and you don't want to, but they symbolize abundance on an affordable table in your home. They're like . . . Exactly. Who cares. And not caring is a huge luxury, not to be taken lightly. Fucker.

I'm telling my good friend down the street that the only thing more fashionable than a pale, thin person who has not yet begun to wrinkle is a pale, thin, unwrinkled person who is not particularly rattled that poets have given up on meaning. And the only thing more fashionable than an unflappable, translucent person is a poem that flies and flies without ever landing. And the only thing more fashionable than a poem that risks dying of exhaustion is a belt, a really nice belt with the steam still rising off it.

My friend says I can come in if I promise not to talk unless she points at me.

I say, there's not much to talk about. There have only ever been two kinds of poetry: narrative and lyric. And some other kind that is sort of lyric but in a new way that sounds like a breakdown but doesn't lead to the hospital because that's a narrative.

She says she had forgotten but she's actually expecting out-of-town company soon.

I say, don't worry: narrative and lyric hate each other, but like the rest of us they share a house and make babies. They buy one another the perfect gifts.

She's making a sandwich because she can't stand to face it.

I continue to confront her. I say, narrative and lyric become one another on sidewalks and passers by are afraid to look. It happens to the best of us.

Does she think I wouldn't like a sandwich?

Narrative is lyric's dog, and I don't mind saying that lyric is beginning to bark and scratch as well.

She takes a bite and then realizes she's got a ninja star in her mouth.

Oh, the Many Ways of Speaking

The tropes, the structures!
The waxed boards of various rhetorics
carrying us high, high onto the shore!

While we remain standing.
And perfectly dry. I might say_____
(something intriguing but ultimately baffling)

but I wouldn't quite know what it meant,
which is a form
of moving beautifully,

of appearing to be
gestating the Christ child.
History is punctuated!

I am plural, unknown to myself!
Yet my salve is right here on the shelf.
When I say _____ (something tailored)

I'm promoted to
the corner office of both of our minds.
But when I say_____

(something bowl-like)
I've been stupid. I'm in humiliating,
French trouble, the moldy part of which

cannot be cut out this time.
Perne in a gyre! Where but to think
is to have your throat

crammed with marshmallow.
And why, when hand signals
are all that's necessary:

this seepage hurts! Bang,
you're the one that's dead. I can't control
my emotions right now! Look

at the disgusting sunrise!
My fucking dove! All night

I will claw this way at the air for you!
The blood of living
will pour into our mouths!

Miss Peach Imagines She Is an Aging British Rock Star and Considers Bipedalism While Responding to a Beautiful Woman Who Has Just Said "I Love You"

"I am just a monkey man,
and I'm glad you are a monkey woman, too, baby."
The Rolling Stones

Sister, if you want to cry, think of the savannah,
the bosom of life gone suddenly flat

over a couple thousand years. Tonight you will trot around

with the starving herd, dressed in bright scraps
of nostalgia for the density of the rain forest. When just to have an arm
was to have an anvil and just to swing it

was to kill something delicious. Come here with that sadness

of endless grasses. I will say this once:
one orangutan could've controlled

and fertilized a population of 400 if we would've
gotten out of the way and let him.
Why did we ever stand up?

There's nothing I hate more than the variety of factors.

It's impossible to say anything and even harder
to shut up. Let's face it: we are always working backwards
from a pile of bones. Don't take that personally.

I think we can agree, at least, that women have legs. And I can relate
to this cruelty, this being lifted off of sheets, being carried away
by a million specialized parts, the head mounted

like a stone that has again escaped the ground

for a time. Human beings get no practice
at staying. We have no special limbs for it. Once we commit
to being still, darling, it's all we ever get to do.

Neighbor(3): Flying after Her

At first they only took away the pieces of her that were loose, but we all know
once the parts are missing it's OK to set the board game on fire.

I saw her yesterday in a tree. Someday I'll find words for the dripping.
Like rain mixed with teeth.

When I was eight she told me she crawled in and out
of her own mouth and often got stuck there.
She said when she looked up to the sun it stopped her from rotting.
It turned her face back to its permanent steel version.
She said, what do you want fixed? Leave it open to the world
because the world is exactly the kind of half-dead thing
a wound can understand. I was a giant then,
and she was the sack of gold I was owed every day.

She always said, why not do the kind of things we wish birds would do?

When something hard is falling from the sky, how do you know it isn't the very piece
you need to complete your face? When it isn't the piece you need, how do you know
your face isn't better off blown apart? When your face isn't better off blown apart,
how do you know who really loves you?

The Pirates of Gold River

Chapter 1

You want a place to keep it, a place for it to be, a repository, a source. For the gold.
The gold you feel all day burning inside you, gaining supernatural value,
threatening the leadership of your head. The gold fighting to display itself in your eyes,
pulling you toward other people, turning the heap of togetherness into something
permanent and musical.

You were mined from a hole in the earth that you belong to like larvae belong
to a honeycomb. We all have a home, but it's a law of dispersal
that not all of us will fit back in it.

To be loose at a time like this is to lose your teeth and be a pirate entering the sun.

Chapter 2

You begin with a town because a town is where it begins. A town is always
lost or buried. It's always obscured by raw mountains. You are always in the dirt
digging it out. Hunter, drifter. Species: marauder. With your thorax boat
and your old face whipping at the top of your sharpened mast. With your forked arms
and your improved relationship with the monsters of the air. Water and dirt
serve dutifully as your two emotions.

Chapter 3

Gold River collapsed on itself, but before that, so did everyone in it.
The hand in front of your face became rapid and disturbing.
So much for the preciousness being stashed in the body.
Eventually our bones became the spoons that stirred us.

Chapter 4

We are safe, the body is ruined.

Chapter 5

The real voyage begins as the joints unlock, every instant a shining hill or valley
beyond ownership—original, unseen, utterly remote and detached from the place
you were a second before. The living room walls are a new form of sea, the sensation
in your knee another box inside a box sinking with its treasure through the silted bottom.
The main island is no longer your head. The self becomes a desperate way of holding on,
of stringing things together, but that's been true for a long, long time.

Chapter 6

A metal city grinds in the distance. His fingers rest in pieces on the seams of her face,
bone on bone. The other option is to turn to jelly.

Chapter 7

When the pirates finally arrived, desiccated and coughing, Gold River was back in full swing.
Strings of lights had been hung between the houses, and the pirates found
that the twinkling festoons were exactly what they'd been missing.

Chapter 8

So you are a polyglot, fluent in water and digging. With no clearly demarcated head,
your hair's no longer sure where it should grow. Sea creature.
You gave up your body and went to live in the foam. You stung people

with spiny ridges that weren't yours, floated up under their chairs
with contagious tentacles. Abyssal plane. You float in and out of your cave
with no arms and legs, newly electric. Your old body bloats in the corner. Harbinger.
Contaminant. You and your kind. Now you want to go home? To be alive?
To have a tiny house, a sweet and personalized explanation, a hole you can swim through
in and out of this world? I don't think so.

Chapter 9

Kindness. A table pulled out under the sun for several generations.

Epilogue

Look at the insanity expressed in the mechanics of the knee.
The winged desperation of the pelvis. The wind passes through
as if through a curtain. What do you think?
Maybe lace. Maybe cut flowers nearby.

Peach

The head, the mouth, the fruit, the eating.
The pit, the teeth, the branch, the falling.
The wet, the swollen, the light, the seeing.
The picking, the washing, the cutting, the quartering.
The sweet, the having.

The holding of it in your hands,
beautiful and then ruined. The forms of devouring. The remaining empty.
What's inside.

The excitement of the definite article. What's inside
one thing is analogous to what's inside another.
The ceremonial names

of what is done to them. What is unknown requires a new way of cutting.
What we're left with.

How we make an object ours, make it disappear.
How we become the object and are food.
How we are delicious and dead at the center in so many ways.
How that is wrong and it is stillness, moon-like at the core.
How what we are is whatever reflects off it. How we are light produced earlier
by other things.

Dance Comes to Gold River

Something deadly started bringing its teeth around.
The earth's pounding crept in
and left a piece of itself in your ear. You were alone

with the banging you do on your own door,
the nowhere and everywhere of yourself
that you have no hope of ever picking up
and looking at. You had to catch the sticky fly

circling above you. It became your heart.
But the arms and legs, they hadn't happened yet.
Until now nothing required tendons. Everything

required sleep. Then something died that wasn't you.
The air laid the scent of blood at your feet,

and you brought a twisted movement like a candle
out of the fog of your body.

The Meeting

They were deep in it and about to vote on what it was.
The leaves above them began to drip and blur
the proceedings. Thumper, Miss Peach, the yellow pile of wax
that was the Candlestick Maker, all of them
batted whatever lashes they had at the middle distance and recited possible recipes
for what was leaking out of their eyes.

The Black Coat read from The Official Complaint:
for years everything has been about itself, the music
about music, the light about light. In the small patch of woods
on the south end of town, someone played with a rock and a feather
and was never seen or heard from again.

3 parts: dirt thrown at the moon   1 part: other people's bodies

Miss Peach straightened her lichen vest, lied down,
and pretended she was dead. Thumper sang a cappella about berries
and knowing what to do, the Black Coat swatted patchy bluebirds
from Miss Peach's eyes. Everyone's mouth craved the irritation of dirt,
but their faces, all mere surface damage and glow,
spoke of more. Of a time when things happened
and led quickly to other things. Of a place
beyond the trunks of trees.

Soon they would lose the light filtering in from the big game down the road. No matter.
They could feel their faces beginning to cave in and didn't need to see.

3 parts: footsteps approaching your nest   1 part: your head held above the crowd
on a satin pillow

1 part: wild mint   2 parts: your mother seeing you walk into a clearing
after you've been dead for so many years

The River (That Is Washing Her Away) Is a Symbol for Seven Things

To the class (that isn't there):

Once we have fully described how the evening arrives
(it steps out of the trees), we can turn
our attention to the area of the tongue
that experiences sourness.

Aside:

The rain is sideways, and Miss Peach a vulnerable powder.
By now a paste.

To the class (in a black dress like a box into which she puts herself):

Men of a certain age, a certain "background." *Shuffle papers.*
They will ("awash," "cloven," "indolent")
ironically detail the, for them, crushingly unknowable streets
of rural France. Rural France will once again
be a stand-in for your tight bottoms, ladies. The irony will once again
be somewhat instructive. (See 20th century, the)
The sense of being crushed will, once again,
be the source of the erotic in the story.

Aside:

Some girls inevitably form a thin paste, a rime of high voices on the stems,
a layer of film over the fronds that seals off the roar coming from the forest.
The quiet wears a human lace.

To the class:

The senses are. We'll leave it at that.

Aside:

What do you cross girls with? Are you kidding? Storms or debris
classically. Telephone poles or trees, depending on the century.
The sounds of a cat unable to deliver her backlog of kittens
because of the design failure of her own body. Links of sausage,
stone-ground flour, a vat of maple. The dust of ultramarine pigment
in the corner of the painter's studio that you shouldn't breath.

Fill out a form, man. Are you going to eat her
or do you want her to burn down your home?
Do you want to die from the inside out or the outside in?
Would you rather have all the smooth, round stones turn into eyes
or have all the eyes turn into smooth, round stones?

To the class:

"To describe" is probably not to "to know"—you're all devils. *Put the chalk down.*

Aside:

My glue. My child. My runny mixture.

You're separating into simple parts. You're in reverse.
Soon the ingredients—baking soda, flour,
the sickness after great laughter—will be back in my hands,
the gasp of revelation will be shoved back down my throat.

To the air above the students' heads:

Not again.

To the class:

If you turn and look out the back window, you can see what some might call a face pressed against the glass.

That Sweet, Sweet Evolution Thing

Sex: mist-shrouded,
rhythmic
island.

Science:
bold canoe.

There are reasons for our strange positions:
the tyranny of the pelvis,
the chance we would become too philosophical and die.

It is the opposite of nails down a chalkboard:
when lovers close their eyes.

Levels of failure:
many.

The worst level:
DNA-level.

If, then:
"I'll show you a fractal!"

The real question:
would we if we could?

Evidence:
history.

Instead I am lucky to have evolved:
hidden sex organs.
(Unlike a cat or the more flamboyant of the monkeys.)

Topics I no longer have questions about:
brain chemicals.

When we do something new:

we fail. (Unless we can do it for so long
we begin to produce new chemicals.) There is, I think:
electricity involved as well.

Miss Peach Gets Lucky

So I had a date with this werewolf. I said I'd give him
a Tuesday dinner slot if he got all his tangles out. After all that

conditioner, he did feel greasy,
but no worse than your average guy
by late Sunday afternoon. And we're supposed to feel sorry

for the frothing one. He's a bleeding wild flower,
a sock that would scratch you raw and doesn't even have a match.
He's got basic desires that lack a corresponding orifice.

And we're a kind people.
We thank our monsters for letting us invent them. They let us feel dignified

and unsutured by comparison. They're the parts of ourselves
we pity only when they're covered in fur, the parts
that never married, never caught a whiff
of their own species, never got out of the house without

severing some plump limb.
So I could've stayed home, but what is the heart
without a few sharp knives around?

I did take precautions. My dress looked as unlike a steak
or any sort of first-degree murder as possible, which meant, of course,
I was swirled like a cupcake.

I climbed into his mouth
not long after we sat down to eat. The tables of people
looked like loose animals
through the bars of his teeth.

I didn't say anything, I wanted to spare his feelings,
but I was disappointed when it didn't hurt.

So now I work for him. My job is to have flesh,
and I'm fairly good at it. He's president

of not ripping my head off. What worthwhile lover
couldn't, though? Love is a fancy name
for giving someone without fangs the power to kill you.

In our bed I lie next to him and his spasmodic changes.
Our bed is a darkness in which we feel
instead of see the stars.

When I hear the *fsssssst* of his tiny hairs parting
and the wet rip of his claws starting to grow, I think, Hey,
which is sharper, teeth or lies,

teeth or lies, baby? The scary monster
is the back of the head, the face you thought you knew, gone,
turned away. Scream all you want to.

How many satisfying meals turn out to be poisonous?
When we love something, isn't it as if we have grown hands

especially to hold it? What have we ever touched
and not had to watch turn ugly
by the light of some sort of moon?

Miss Peach by the Sea

In a world of dubious oysters,
Miss Peach is not the bucket you lurch toward,
not the team of medics who graze you
like wings and carry only needles that go in, like true love,
on the first try. She might be the sand
grinding against your teeth.
She might be the smell on your fingers
no amount of lemon can clean.
All we know for certain is that
she's not what made you sick,
not what almost killed you,
but she is what first made you think
something was going to.

The Musicians of Gold River

Two boys worry about clarinets, about their efficiency,
the emotions people have for them.

Why is the fiddle the most beautiful instrument? It represents defeat
and a longing for home. What doesn't? We have limited ourselves needlessly

and should make a new instrument every day. Wind across
what materials will express the tone of endless Kansas

in this proud and faded skirt hem? What does it mean to evoke
what is already here stealing our dignity?

The making of instruments becomes a type of music
while the grass overtakes the once well-appointed manor.

The boys' fingers seemed to leave burns on one another's skin,
tiny bright injuries but nothing wrong. No marks anywhere.

Very much like notes. Very much. Let them know
how long they will walk down the hallway before they can expect me

to come into view. Like kings, like great imperial rulers, like we all were
back in the days when we believed in materiality so deeply

everything shone like gold, they will be compensated, rewarded
for solving the riddle of our endless disappointment.

Neighbor(4): Miss Peach Belongs

back in her mother's arms, not sprawled on the ground beside a picnic table.
Can someone please at least bring me a drink of water? What I'm looking for
is a state of such abundant presence it will be experienced as blankness.
Her swollen head is all that's left. 50, 60 lbs. easy. Can someone please bring me
the undiminished data of a life, a pulsing and towering wall? My shoulder
finally gives out after an hour of propping her up to talk and eat. I want to be
surrounded and I used to think it didn't matter by what. I collected glass for a while,
thought a lot about how the future supercharges the present. Nothing sadder
than a metaphor, though people do soak into objects. She's addressing the issue
of how one feels muscular when rowing a boat which illuminates the real issue
of not having hands. Of course someone else has dislocated her elbow and we have
another animal story on the tennis court. Your own and other people's pain
can heighten detail but too much and the day is a wash of hormones, by which I mean
the public park does not return to its solid form once it's been converted to a gas.
We're way past judging one another for having no real innate behaviors. We're not sure
what she could be choking on. We're willing to watch it happen—involuntary
movement is mesmerizing like a snake—but we're not willing to let it have happened.
We attach to the moments like crystals which converts the air into sheets of ice.
This is glass. This is a truly new world that cannot be walked on. No form of waking
has been invented here. Instead of time we have her skin.

Summary, with Winter Berries

Miss Peach is Julia Roberts.
Miss Peach is the act of getting out of bed in the morning.

Miss Peach gets stuck with pins.
Miss Peach: head of an eagle.

Miss Peach is unclearly packaged.
Miss Peach is the glue we used as toothpaste.

Miss Peach is the conflict we have in winter
holding plump, white berries.

Miss Peach's tiny, smashed face is so dear.
Miss Peach lives in the woods and embodies betrayal.

Variorum

At least most of the violence has been off the page.
Most of the violence, at least, has been kept off the page.
Most of the violence takes place off the page, as is always the case.
None of the violence is ever on the page.
Violence is never on the page.
The violence thus far has primarily taken place off the page.
The violence thus far has been implied.
For the most part, the violence is not on the page.
For the most part, the page is not violent.
The page really can't be violent. At least.
The page, for the most part, takes place off the page!
At least the violence. At least for the most part.
As usual, for the most part, as is always the case.
As usual, most violence happens off the page.
As usual, the page. Mostly the violence.

Miss Peach: A Historical Reenactment

Once Upon a Time involves a horse. It involves
      an outlying moor and a young woman riding a horse
until she grows parched. Her parching
      makes her pale, her paleness makes her weak,
her weakness makes her beautiful, etc....

Her beauty invariably knocks her down
      not far from a country inn. The shy but merry people
who churn and pick and thread in the town
      watch her through dirty windows. They are a small people;
their sons, though, are large. They tell us

what it's like to be large in a country
      of smallness. They turn toward the rose bush and have it
blush for them. For one son in particular,
      time stands in pieces like a forest to be chopped.
He is strong enough, though,

to stand in one place forever, swinging,
      holding an enormous weight. She dreams of being
that weight. She becomes lopsided, stone-like,
      and more and more beautiful on the side of her body
that faces the direction of his leafy cottage home.

She begins to ride in circles. He begins
      to live at the gate. We know that his dumbness
is really kindness and that sometimes
      it makes her faint, but otherwise the story
gets patchy at this point. One evening,

despite the stink in the back pen,
        she is seen covered in dirt, stroking his hair. His face
is said to have taken on an expression
        variously described as "winged," "tinseled," and "consumed."
It was one of those days

when the sky fills with white petals,
        as if even the trees were letting go. Someone found a piece of paper
with the word "Constantine" in her handwriting.
        There's a rumor of a stone carried like a child. Someone
of his description is said to have stolen a ship

or died a beggar. Her last known words
        and several streets in Paris, when pronounced while sobbing,
sound the same.

Neighbor(5): Miss Peach Is Real

To find something beautiful one must have no idea
what it is.

The skin warbles.
We all become the throats of birds disappearing
under the sea. I had no idea, for example,

that this display of metal was my wedding. How I loved
the shining chairs no one could sit in, the hilarious but lovely uselessness
of what we've made.

All my years of knifey girls were there with their caustic ribs,
their hairpin poses, their actual hair dark with hatred.
They got drunk and blew my mind:
it sucks to be them! The body is a thousand arrows
pointing at itself. We laughed together like children

with the same bad parents. The sweetness after the parade
of overconfidence is unbearable.
We still have hearts. My god, we need each other. And her,
the most pretend one,
now that you mention it, in white, and me,
dissolved almost completely but around here somewhere.
Though it was unofficial, I drew her rag-like into my mouth
and made off to the beginning-of-time cave.

Miss Peach: The Novel

Hook: she's back in town after spending
the last several centuries in the form

of endless sand. Turns out everyone wishes
they'd hurt her when she was young and sprawled

in the grass. Brave insights here into the violence
latent in all sexual encounters. She buys the local

lunch spot, and one night at the drive-in,
they get their chance. Opening: *Gold River, 2000.*

As they clap for their sons spitting into the dust of the dry
August field, nobody sees the blood on their hands.

Except she has sunstruck tentacles and her eyes
are a rare type of wings. New opening: *Fairytale 2000.*

Everyone in Glorywood has a slight fever. Except of course
the tentacles are toxic to asthmatic children

and aren't real: *Sharon Brugler had a doctor's appointment*
at noon that she didn't want her husband Hal to know about.

Followed by seven pages of circular logic about horse evolution.
Incident involving the 1950s, wholeness, mathematics,

and the lines of a wingback chair. The sun is closer
on Borgonia, which means no mirrors. She has no idea

she's beautiful until either her half brother touches her
or she kills someone and confronts her image as she wades

into the sick, sick water, implicating no less than
the earth itself. Many allusions. A passage connecting

a series of goat sacrifices in ancient Greece to the way she feels
about the light catching her hairbrush. Her sisters think

they know everything and represent systems theory.
Everyone is diagnosed with serious history. When she says "Jared"

it represents America. The characters meet each other near the end
in tiny boats in the middle of the ocean. Each has one part

of an oar. Imagery throughout of fishhooks and tiny soaps.
Repeated but subtle mentions of the gills of the devil. The world,

recognizable even under the thick layer of gelatin,
hovers inches away too repulsive to be touched.

Miss Peach, American

I was uneasy at first about how much
I loved myself, but I had to show the rest of you

how to do it. On Friday nights,
I pondered the tip of the iceberg
that was my smile. But I was alone in the big TV room.

I had the soft, fuzzy couch
to myself, so to speak. I felt a little gooey,
a little cross-eyed, like I was eating
a big bowl of myself with me syrup and me sprinkles
and me nuts and lots of marshmallow. It was fine,

except when it wasn't. There comes a point in every life
that actually does draw blood. So I started
having dinner parties. I posted signs,

and someone came. He said he lived down the street
and it was true. He had no problems
with his dad or his face
or the sheer, violent number of women in the world.
No empty feeling around windows. So for the next couple weeks,
on Tuesdays and Fridays after ten,

I became what was left
when he couldn't get anymore down.

I was dropped and spread and ultimately
caked into the floorboards. I was a bowl
for which there was no appropriate spoon.

I was a convenience, right up there
with Coke and Diet Coke. That powerful. That full
of sugar or completely devoid of sugar.
I left terrible stains. It sounds

unsanitary, and it was.
I was a convincing reason to get sick
of a house altogether and just move, move
because, look, there's stuff here
that cannot be cleaned. Even so,

I missed the mouth
when it went away. We all do. Like life,
it had a particular openness to it
that I liked being crammed into.

Nothing Is Ever Missing in Gold River

As I arrive, sometime
between 5:30 and 6:00, only a slow-moving softness

remains on the grass. Another world

was resting here
and has just left.

The air clings to its brightness as if it could turn the brightness into a ship
and leave as well. In the orange glow

much is revealed: this parting moment
is what trees have always eaten.

Everything anyone here ever wanted
turns out to be a quality of light.

The Stranger Manual

Try having a home exclamatory with lit windows and try
to be what is lighting those windows. Try new curtains. Try to be
what is new about the curtains.

Make sure you have a home. You're going to want
to hurt yourself a little inside of something you own.

Sooner or later you become a winged creature, a whirring sound. You are the powder
that made the wings work until the fire became your whole head.
Your house is the enormous, upright state of flying.
Your ownership of it is the glow
disappearing behind the rising, castle-like dome of your thorax.

Each day is a section in your endless abdomen.
You're a unit of time, a greeting, an oxidized bead,
the body hung in the air and infested
with the buzz of life. Your instructions
will be carried to the four corners of the earth,
though they will alter slowly and become unrecognizable.

You will become unrecognizable. Strange wing markings.
You will land on a window and be called Atlas, Luna, Virgin Tiger,
on a door and be Eyes of the Sphinx. Hush.
Can you hear? Microscopic pieces of your face
are being eaten in the shadows of great mountains.

Miss Peach Imagines She Is an Aging British Rock Star and Considers What Is Essential in Life While Responding to a Beautiful Woman Who Has Just Said "I Love You"

The throat is not optional.
Neither is the liver or the brain.

Who cares about things that come in pairs,
about things that can be viably removed.

The goal of life is to make the world
precious, or at least one thing in it.

I keep living on without things:
parents, lovers, Indonesian coins.

True, I can't stop staring at the branches as they reveal
the cracks and general devastation lurking in the air.

Image of sadness.
But sadness has its pleasures.

You can walk while you are doing it.
You can feel your remaining bones

gliding effortlessly, not needing
any socket they don't already have.

Like wind in a cave, my love,
like many winds in many, many caves.

A Food We Once Ate Is Mentioned By Name

And we are filled with a fog-like discontent.
And we are unsure of even the personal value of our observations.
It's as if we're asking one another to sleep in small beds built for children.
It's as if by walking we're disfiguring those underground.
Being present at the initial event was deemed unsafe in October 2000.
Being present was like holding sparklers that wouldn't go out.
When we lost Gold River, the trees became metaphysical and our brains wooden.
When we forgot our families' faces, we became more lovely at sunset like a toxic cloud.
Dogs were everywhere, sniffing and tracking, and a wonderful thing happened.
Dogs were nudging us to get up, it was wet, we looked down, and a wonderful thing happened.

Afterward, new role models better demonstrated not knowing those we love.
Afterward, with needles, we made our symbiosis more frankly biological.
Once again our former home is preserved inside the mountain on which we've awakened.
Once again each speck of dirt is a frontier.
What will be tossed down the well?
What will be the first words of the covenant because that's all we'll remember?
The dead and the living hang from each moment like bats.
The dead and the living are a pattern that can be hummed.
Now even I am being held in someone's arms and it turns out the river is a type of bone.
Now even the dead, when seen up close, turn out to be moving.

Acknowledgments

Thank you to the editors of the magazines and anthologies in which these poems appeared, sometimes under different titles and in other forms:

Alaska Quarterly Review: "New Year's Eve"
American Letters and Commentary: "A Rose Is a Rose Is a Rose Is Miss Peach"
American Poetry Review: "All Objects Reveal Something about the Body" and "Peach"
Antioch Review: "What Will Become of This Tension"
Barrelhouse: "Miss Peach by the Sea"
Bluckbird: "The Monkey Whose Job It Used to Be to Sit on Miss Peach's Shoulder Takes Up Olde Timey Music"
Black Warrior Review: "Neighbor (2): Miss Peach in Velvet"
Boston Review: "A Food We Once Ate Is Mentioned by Name" and "Miss Peach: The Novel"
Crazyhorse: "Doctor (2): Miss Peach Visits the Rural Walk-in Clinic" and "Neighbor (1): Miss Peach's Body Didn't Turn Out Right"
Diagram: "The Pirates of Gold River," "The River (That Is Washing Her Away) Is a Symbol for Seven Things," and "The Wondering Class"
Drunken Boat: "In Defense of the Prince of Gold River," "Neighbor (3): Flying after Her," "Neighbor (4): Miss Peach Belongs," and "The Prince of Gold River on the Imposition of the Galactic"
The Gettysburg Review: "Gold River," "The Musicians of Gold River," and "That Sweet, Sweet Evolution Thing"
Gulf Coast: "Miss Peach Is Real" and "The Stranger Manual"
The Iowa Review: "Miss Peach Returns to High School to Retake Driver's Ed" and "Doctor (3): Miss Peach Is Referred to the Orthopedic Unit"
The Kenyon Review Online: "New York, New York, New York, New York, New York"
LIT: "Summary, with Winter Berries"
New Ohio Review: "Miss Peach Imagines She Is an Aging British Rock Star and Considers the Human Condition While Responding to a Beautiful Woman Who Has Just Said, 'I Love You'" and "The Meeting"
Prairie Schooner: "Dance Comes to Gold River" and "Winter in Gold River"
Pleiades: "Miss Peach Is a Doll inside a Doll inside a Doll," "Miss Peach, Female Impersonator" "Miss Peach, American," and "Miss Peach: The War Years"

Ploughshares: "Miss Peach Is a Cross Between" and "Miss Peach and the Problem of
    Human Beauty"
River Styx: "Love, with Trees and Lightning" and "Miss Peach Gets Lucky"
Seneca Review: "Gold River Is Never Really on Fire," "Miss Peach Pierces the Vale," and
    "Things That Didn't Work"
The Southern Review: "Miss Peach: A Historical Reenactment," "Miss Peach Goes
    Shopping," "Miss Peach Imagines She Is an Aging British Rock Star and Explains
    What Honesty Is," and "Miss Peach Explains Promiscuity to a Toddler"
Verse: "A Poem about Poetry by Miss Peach, Hobo/Provocateur," "Monday in Gold River,"
    and "Oh, the Many Ways of Speaking"

"Miss Peach Visits Her Ex-Boyfriends in the Hospital" and "Miss Peach Imagines
    She Is an Aging British Rock Star and Considers What Is Essential in Life While
    Responding to a Beautiful Woman Who Has Just Said 'I Love You'" appeared in
    Poetry 30: Thirty Poets in Their Thirties (Mammoth Books, 2005).

"Love, with Trees and Lightning" also appeared in *Isn't It Romantic: 100 Love Poems by
    Young American Poets* (Wave Books, 2004).

"All Objects Reveal Something about the Body" was commissioned by Julia Ritter for the
    Julia Ritter Performance Group as text to accompany choreography in *Odd Sympathies
    (Something Just Happened to Me)*.

Thank you to Jo Carney, David Blake, and all my friends and colleagues at The College
of New Jersey and to The National Endowment for the Arts for their support and for the
time that made this book possible. Thank you to Jeffrey Shotts and Katie Dublinski along
with everyone else at Graywolf Press and to my patient, thoughtful readers and friends
all of whom left their mark on this book, especially Jon Baker, Amy Benson, Iris Berets,
Steve Langan, Julia Ritter, Nathan Roberts, and Taije Silverman. Thank you to my
teacher Thomas Rabbitt and to my family—Lynn, Robert, Jane, Stephen, Annie, David,
Carrie, Colin, Ian, and Izzy.

In memory of C. Douglas Fix

Catie Rosemurgy is the author of *My Favorite Apocalypse*. She teaches at The College of New Jersey and lives in Philadelphia.

This book was designed by Rachel Holscher. It is set in Goudy Old Style type by Bookmobile Design & Digital Publisher Services, and manufactured by Bookmobile on acid-free paper.